Supplies

PAINTS

Delta Ceramcoat® Acrylic Paints

Delta Ceramcoat® Gleams™, 14K Gold

DecoArt™ Easy Blend Stencil Paint™ (dry-brush formula), Calico Red

Please refer to individual projects for specific colours, or to the colour swatches on page 28.

BRUSHES

Brushes must be in good condition to achieve good results. It is impossible to do nice brush strokes with a poor brush.

LOEW-CORNELL
LA CORNEILLE® GOLDEN TAKLON

Series JS Jackie Shaw Liner: #2

Series 7000 Round: #0 or #1, #3 or #4

Series 7300 Shader (Flat): #4, #8, #10 and #12

Series 7350 Liner: #2/0 or smaller

Series 7550 Wash/Glaze: 3/4"

Series 7850 Deerfoot Stippler: 1/8" and 1/4"

MISCELLANEOUS

Series 2014 Round Bristle Scumbler (size determined by what is comfortable for you)

Mop brush (optional, for softening colour)

Old flats or foam brushes (for basecoating)

OTHER SUPPLIES

Brown paper bag (for sanding)

Chalk pencil (gray or white Conte or equivalent)

Clapham's Beeswax Salad Bowl Finish (optional)

Cotton swabs (inexpensive, non-fuzzy kind)

Delta Ceramcoat All-Purpose Sealer

Delta Ceramcoat Artist Gesso (optional)

Delta Ceramcoat Brush Cleaner or a bar of pure soap

Delta Ceramcoat Color Float™ (optional)

Delta Ceramcoat Extender (optional)

Delta Ceramcoat Gel Stain Medium

Delta Ceramcoat Sparkle Glaze™

Delta Ceramcoat Waterbase Varnish, matte or satin

Hair dryer

Isopropyl (rubbing) alcohol

Kneaded eraser

Krylon #1311 Matte Finish Spray Coating

Loew-Cornell Brush Tub®

Loew-Cornell Fine Line Painting Pen (optional)

Masking tape

Masking tape, low-tack

Metal primer (your choice of brand)

Palette knife

Palette pad (for acrylics)

Paper towels

Pencil, hard-lead

Plastic wrap

Ruler

Sandpaper, fine

Small bottle cap (for water)

Stylus

Tack cloth or a damp, lint-free cloth

Tracing paper

Transfer paper (white and gray)

Vinegar

White shellac (available at any paint or hardware store)

Wood filler

Sources

Stone Bridge Collection
R.R. 4, Pakenham, ON K0A 2X0 Canada
107 Court Street, Watertown, NY 13601 USA
Phone: (613) 624-5080   Fax: (613) 624-5081
Toll-free order line: (800) ART-TOLE
Web site: www.stonebridgecoll.com

"Blueberry Fairy" and "Wild Strawberry Fairy" scalloped heart plate WD1451; "Celebration!" pressed wood plate WD1011; "Blue Fairies" scoop plate WD1417; "Baking Fairies" breadboard WD1050; "Poppy Fairy" pressed wood plate WD1010; Clapham's Beeswax Salad Bowl Finish

Walnut Hollow
1409 State Road 23
Dodgeville, WI 53533
Phone: (800) 950-5101
Web site: www.walnuthollow.com

"Little Apple Fairy" oval tray #3564

Viking Woodcrafts, Inc.
1317 8th Street SE
Waseca, MN 56093
Phone: (800) 328-0166   Fax: (507) 835-3895
E-mail: viking@vikingwoodcrafts.com
Web site: www.vikingwoodcrafts.com

"Blueberry Fairy" hurricane lamp #109-1023 and shade #109-1017; "Celebration!" ornaments: bulb-shaped #20-10522 and teardrop #20-10521; "Baking Fairies" recipe box #20-9595 and note holder #20-10534; "Little Apple Fairy" antique box #43-0010 and papier-mâché teakettle #35-9370; "Poppy Fairy" galvanized water pitcher #164-1023

General Instructions

WOOD PREPARATION

If you are using pressed wood plates, similar to the ones used here, or if using MDF (Medium Density Fiber) board, there is no need to seal because the wood is very dense, non-porous and does not contain excess sap; but do sand after the first coat of paint. For other types of wood, however, follow the instructions below.

Fill any nail holes with wood filler. Sand with the grain, then remove dust with a tack cloth or damp, lint-free cloth. Treat for tannin where necessary (see note below). Seal wood, applying *one* coat, unless otherwise specified. When dry, sand surface with fine sandpaper. Remove dust and apply a basecoat when instructed. If you wish to stain your piece, and if it is not necessary to treat wood first for tannin (such as with the pressed wood plates), you may apply stain directly to the wood.

NOTE: I have had bad experiences with tannin damage on some of my earlier work, and have seen those same problems on other artists' projects. This seems to be a problem with pine pieces, in particular. Not only the tannin in the obvious knots has come through, but some wood has sappy grain that also bleeds through the paint. Now I treat those suspect areas first with white shellac, before sealing. If the wood on the project is going to be basecoated, you could use a stain-blocking primer, which is available in paint stores.

Always prepare all surfaces, leaving no wood unfinished. Wood is porous and is affected by humidity. When moisture gets in, wood expands and then shrinks as it dries.

NOTE: In the project instructions, I have not always repeated the directions for sanding and removing dust. It should always be the normal procedure.

METAL PREPARATION

Wash the metal object first with soap and water, and then with a strong solution of vinegar and water. Rinse with clean water. Place in a 200-degree oven to dry thoroughly, or air dry for a few days. It takes time for the seams to dry.

Spray with metal primer. Let dry about three days (or according to instructions on the paint can) before basecoating.

BACKGROUND BASECOAT

Use a foam brush or a basecoat brush of your choice to apply two or three even coats of base colour. Allow each coat to dry, then "sand" with a piece of brown paper bag.

APPLYING STAIN

I generally prefer applying water-based stain with a damp cloth. You may use a brush and then wipe away excess with a cloth, but I find that using only a damp cloth results in a lighter, more even application.

TRANSFERRING PATTERNS

Trace pattern onto tracing paper using a sharp, hard-lead pencil. Be accurate, especially with faces. Trim your traced pattern to fit the project; also snip a piece off at the top or side to expose some of your project's surface. Place a piece of masking tape lengthwise along the cut edge to make sure it won't shift. It would be helpful to be able to leave the pattern attached, turning it aside while basecoating the design components, and then returning it back to the exact position to add details.

NOTE: Before you start transferring the pattern, make sure that your basecoat is completely dry. The tape might lift the paint from your surface if it is still damp. People often complain that transfer lines are very hard to remove, and I have had the same trouble myself. The main reason lines do not erase is because transferring was done before the surface was allowed to dry completely. If you can't erase the lines, try removing them with a cloth, slightly dampened with mineral spirits or turpentine. The thin setting lines (see "Definition of Terms") might come off too, so be careful.

When the pattern is secured, slip transfer paper underneath. (Use gray for light backgrounds and white for dark backgrounds. Exception: I have discovered that with some brands of white transfer paper, the lines will show on white or Light Ivory backgrounds.) Make sure you have the coated side down. Use a stylus or a sharp, hard-lead pencil to lightly transfer the pattern. If you press too hard, you will leave an indentation in the wood and it will be hard to erase graphite lines. Test your pressure by transferring only a small area, then lifting up the pattern and transfer paper to see how dark your lines are. If the lines are too dark, erase lightly with a kneaded eraser to prevent them from showing through your strokework.

First, transfer only outlines, omitting detail that will be painted after basecoating an area. You might make an exception when transferring hair. It is a good idea to transfer some of the hair detail to use as directional lines for basecoating (I use form-following strokes to basecoat hair). The brush strokes remain visible, and detail can be painted without having to transfer again. Some of the patterns have small lines indicating shading. Do not transfer those lines.

FINISHING

Erase all remaining transfer lines. Let the paint cure for a day. (Mediums slow down the drying time. If medium was used, let the projects dry a little longer.)

Apply three or more coats of water-base varnish, matte or satin.

NOTE: Do not sand until after the third or fourth coat; otherwise you could damage the painting. Even then, you should be careful. (I could tell you a story about that!!)

PAINTING STRIPES AND BORDERS

People often comment on my borders and think that it takes a very steady hand to do them. Actually, my method (actually an old carpenter's trick) is quite simple and, with a little practice, most people can do it.

Practice first with a pencil on a paper pad or on a piece of scrap wood. (Make sure the edge is smooth so you won't get a splinter or cut your finger.) Set the point of the pencil down on the surface. Place the ring finger of the hand holding the pencil next to the pad. Holding your finger steady, run your finger towards you along the edge of the pad or wood, moving the pencil along with it. The width of the drawn margin is adjusted by holding the pencil at different angles. The finger following along the edge should be in a comfortable position for you.

It's a little different when using a brush. Instead of the ring finger, you use your "pinkie" as the guide along the edge. For stripes with a liner brush, hold the brush almost upright and pull towards you. Reload the brush when needed, being careful when joining lines. For longer, continuous strokes, you can thin your paint with a flow medium.

For broad, painted borders, use a flat brush. (I prefer #12.) First, establish a guide line by using the carpenter's trick and a chalk pencil. Then, with the brush handle pointing toward 3 o'clock (for "lefties" 9 o'clock), pull the chisel edge of the brush toward you along the guide line, pressing the bristles flat against the surface. (It's not a good idea to use your best brush to do this, because you are actually pulling the brush sideways and it might lose its shape. Turn brush occasionally to prevent that.) When you have an even inner edge, it's easy to fill in the rest of the border. Avoid leaving ridges.

When the border is to be left unpainted, and the colour is to be in the centre of the piece, the inner edge of the border can be painted with the colour for the centre using two different methods—outline it with a liner brush first, or pull a flat brush (handle pointing toward 6 o'clock) with one corner of the brush following the guide line. In both cases, let the "pinkie" guide your hand.

BRUSH CARE

Taking care of your brushes is as important as learning the strokes. Everything depends on the condition and quality of your brushes. Misusing a brush, even once, can ruin it because it was not cared for properly.

HERE ARE SOME "DO'S AND DO NOT'S" ABOUT BRUSH CARE:

Never leave a brush in water, even if your water container has slots that suggest that you can. The water will be drawn up the ferrule and can cause damage.

Never twirl a brush around and around when loading or cleaning it. Stroke it in one direction only.

Never leave the brush leaning against the bristles. Even when the brush is left flat on the table, make sure the bristles are not touching anything. Synthetic brushes don't have "memory": once the bristles are misshapen, they don't spring back, even when wet.

Always clean your brush well—it's better to clean it too much than not enough. I tell my students to clean their brush until they think it's clean and then clean it some more. It's surprising how much paint is still in it. Rinse the brush often during each painting session. When finished, rinse brush and then pull the bristles across a bar of soap (or use liquid soap or brush cleaner). Pinch the bristles flat between your thumb and index finger to work out all the paint lodged in the ferrule. Repeat until no colour appears. If you would rather not use your fingers in the cleaning process, gently tap the flat side of the brush against the palette, and then turn it over to do the other side.

Always return the brush to original shape before putting it away—simply reshape the bristles with your fingers.

Do *not* use your best stroke brushes for basecoating. Foam brushes are good for large areas and an old flat shader for smaller ones.

*NOTE: If paint has dried in the brush, the only thing that **might** restore the brush is alcohol (isopropyl rubbing alcohol or vodka.) It is best not to use it too often because it has a drying effect on the bristles. Alcohol might also save clothing that has a spot of paint on it; try it first in an inconspicuous place to make sure of colourfastness.*

A LITTLE ABOUT COLOUR

I am very fortunate to have all the colours of the Ceramcoat line. That makes me too lazy to want to mix colours. It is so easy to open a bottle and pour out just the right colour.

For your convenience, I have included colour swatches of the colours I used. From this chart you can mix or substitute your own colours to match mine, if you wish. Please note that photography and printing processes change the colours somewhat; the pictures of the projects might not look exactly like the real samples. It really is not important for the colours to be exactly the same, as long as the effect is similar. Some people also like to be original and change the colour scheme altogether.

DEFINITION OF TERMS

COLOUR-TO-COLOUR FLOAT (sometimes called a "flip-float"): This is a good technique to use when highlighting and shading the centre of an area. Sideload the brush with the shading or highlighting colour. With the colour side of the brush facing the centre of the area, float a stroke first one way, and then flip the brush over and float a stroke next to the first stroke (colour to colour). Slightly overlap the centre (for a smoother blend), and repeat this technique until the strokes are nicely blended.

This can also be done with a doubleloaded brush. Load one side of the brush with basecoat colour and the other side with highlighting or shading colour. Blend on palette, and apply with highlighting or shading colour facing the centre. This technique also works very effectively when applied in a circle to the middle of a rounded object. Go over lightly to blend. Sometimes my students find it helpful to use a mop brush to very lightly touch or "fluff" the area to achieve a smoother blend.

DOUBLELOADING: Pick up a different colour of paint on each corner of a dampened flat brush. Blend on the palette, first one side of the brush until the two colours blend in the middle; then flip the brush over and blend. Repeat the loading process until you get enough paint in the brush. Blend in the same place on the palette for each load until the paint starts to dry, then start again in another place. Try to keep the colours true in the corners of the brush while maintaining the blended colour in the middle.

DRYBRUSHING: A scumbler, deerfoot stippler or any stiff brush can be used for drybrushing. Pick up paint with a dry brush, and then wipe off excess on a paper towel. There should be very little paint left in the brush. Gently rub the brush in a circular motion on the surface, leaving fine, soft colour.

(Continued on Page 6)

General Instructions
(Continued from Page 5)

FLICK LEAVES: These are the tiny leaves growing here and there from the stems in projects throughout the book. Using a liner or a flat brush, pick up colour, press down on the surface and lift up right away. If using a flat brush, turn the brush a little as you are lifting.

FLOATING COLOUR: I have often used the term "float" in the instructions. This is a technique that uses a side-loaded flat brush to lightly float colour across the surface. (Actually, this can be done with a round brush—and some people do—but I prefer a flat brush.) Floating is used for shading, highlighting and applying transparent layers of colour. Use the largest brush possible for the area that you are painting. It is easier to blend the colour in a large brush than in a small one.

Rinse the brush in water and then blot it on a paper towel until the shine disappears. *NOTE: I use Color Float in the water.* Pick up paint on one corner of the brush and blend on the palette until you see a nice gradation of colour that fades away before it reaches the other corner. If there is even a hint of colour in that "clean" corner, clean the brush and start again. If the colour travels too quickly across the brush, you have too much water in it.

The width and density of the floated colour can be controlled by the amount of paint you pick up, as well as how you blend it on the palette. For a wide shaded (or highlighted) area, pick up a little more paint and "walk" the brush back and forth slightly on the palette to widen the float. For a tiny shaded (or highlighted) area, pick up just a speck of paint and blend only once or twice before applying. It takes some practice to get the feel of it, but be patient and you will be rewarded.

When shading, always start first with a LIGHT application of colour. You can always float subsequent layers to darken, if necessary.

I sometimes darken one side of the design area (such as clothing or berries) a little more, but I keep the shading away from the edge to leave a lighter outline.

TIP: I use the clean corner of the brush to smooth out unwanted, harsh edges where necessary. After using it for that purpose, blot it with a paper towel and add just a little more water to it.

OPAQUE: Solid, even colour (opposite of transparent).

SETTING DETAIL: To prevent transfer lines from showing through a transparent colour, establish or mark the detail or outlines before painting. I use this technique mostly for the face or wing detail, but it can be used anywhere there is danger of transfer lines showing through. Use very thin paint in the colour specified or in the colour to be used over it. For faces, it is all right to paint right on the transferred line, but elsewhere, paint the fine line just inside the transferred line. Erase transfer lines with a soft eraser.

STIPPLING: Stippling is useful for shrubbery, backgrounds for flowers, faux finishes or just to add a bit of texture. Using a deerfoot stippler brush, pick up paint and pounce on the palette a few times before applying to the painting surface, also with a pouncing motion. If a softer look is required, blot excess paint on a paper towel.

SWEEPING: Load the brush with one colour and pull from the side of the puddle of another colour with the tip of the brush.

TINT: My definition of the word is thin, floated colour added over another colour to tint it like frost "tints" leaves in the fall.

TIPPING: Load the brush with one colour, then dip the tip, corner or chisel edge into another colour to paint nice, variegated strokework.

"WALKING" THE BRUSH: This is used to widen the shaded or highlighted area when painting and when adjusting the blend of colours on the palette. It can be done with a side-loaded or doubleloaded brush. With each stroke, move the brush a fraction away from the previous stroke or toward it.

WASH: This is a very thin, transparent layer of colour applied over another colour to give it a different hue.

WET-ON-WET: While the second coat of the base colour is still wet, stroke in another colour and blend. I pick up the second colour on the corner of the brush. Because your surface area is still damp, it's easier to gently smooth out any hard edges of colour.

TIPS

Before starting a project, carefully read all the way through the instructions, and then follow them step-by-step during painting.

When drawing or painting eyes, always start with the eye farthest from your hand; right-handed people start with the left eye and left-handed people start with the right eye. It's easier to line up and match the eyes when you're not covering one or the other with your hand.

Keep a small bottle cap on your palette for a handy water container when painting. It's easier to control the amount of water you pick up when you can see both the water and your brush clearly. For floating, I suggest adding one or two drops of Delta Ceramcoat Color Float to the water in the cap to help achieve a smoother application.

If, after all the love and care, you end up with a brush with bristles that flare out, don't throw it away! It will make a wonderful stippling brush or it can even be used for basecoating.

I have no patience when it comes to waiting for sealers, paints and varnishes to dry. Using a hair dryer will speed up the drying time (use a low setting). I have one on the table beside me at all times.

You need good, direct light when painting. It is especially important when painting small details. I have a drafting lamp directly over my work to eliminate any shadows.

It is best to use an artist brush for varnishing. Any good size brush will work well as long as the bristles are soft. Foam brushes tend to make the varnish foam, whereas an artist brush will allow the varnish to "level" more smoothly and evenly.

CAUTION: When using spray varnishes, do the spraying outdoors, if possible. Sprays contain dangerous toxic fumes.

Painting Faces and Bodies

All the faces in this book have no specific light source. Painting progresses similarly for all of them.

Trace pattern accurately onto tracing paper. Having a pattern on transparent paper is especially important because after basecoating a design area, you will need to reposition the pattern on the painting surface to transfer detail.

It will take three to four coats of paint to basecoat skin areas, especially on dark backgrounds. For small faces, try using a #3 or #4 round brush flattened on the palette; used as a flat brush, it might give you better coverage. Dry between coats and "sand" with a piece of brown paper bag, if necessary. Avoid leaving ridges; thinning the paint slightly for the last coats will give a smoother finish. Dry thoroughly. If the basecoat is not completely dry, the transfer lines will be very hard to remove.

Position the pattern again and transfer detail, preferably with an old piece of transfer paper. If using a new one, wipe first with a paper towel to remove excess graphite. This should not affect its longevity. Use a sharp, hard-lead pencil (2H or harder) to trace the lines for faces as this is more accurate than a stylus. Trace again around the face as well and touch up any differences that may have occurred while basecoating. Set (establish) the detail by lightly painting over the transferred lines with thin shading colour. *NOTE: Color should be so light that you can barely see it.* When dry, erase graphite lines from skin areas.

Shading is done by floating colour with a flat brush. I use a #8 flat for the smaller faces and a #12 for larger ones. That might seem too large, but only one corner is used for colour, leaving the other corner clean for softening and blending when needed. Pick up a tiny bit of paint in the corner of the brush and then stroke a few times on the palette. The small, sharper shadows (like the flares of the nose) are done by picking up just a tiny speck of colour and blending only once or twice on the palette. Each face is a little different and you can follow the colour worksheets to see where shadows are placed. You will also find written step-by-step instructions for placement of shading. Repeat the shading process, drying between layers, until you are satisfied with the result. Floating lightly with the specified red colour on the shading gives life and glow to the skin.

"Eyes are the mirrors of the soul," they say. The eyes really are an important feature on the face. Make sure they line up and are relative in size. In many of the projects they are simplified, with no detail. In the ones that do have detail, dab Light Ivory (or specified colour) on the tiny triangles of the "whites" of the eyes. Paint the irises the colour indicated, making sure they are both looking in the same direction. Pupils are painted using the darkest colour in the palette, with a light-coloured dot for highlight.

Eyebrows are tiny, fine strokes of individual hairs painted in their growth direction, slightly wider towards the centre of the face and tapering into nothing on the sides.

Lips are sometimes very soft and sometimes more colourful. When filling them in, try to cover up the setting line and do not add an outline. Add a little highlight on top of the lower lip where indicated.

Apply shading to other skin areas by first shading around all edges. I sometimes darken one side a little more, keeping the second shading away from the edge, leaving a lighter outline. Where there is overlapping of design components, shade the area underneath. Add detail, like shading to delineate elbow, wrist, ankle and collar bones, etc.

All the liner work is done with a light or medium brown (colour specified in the instructions), and touched up with a dark brown where indicated. There should be no continuous, harsh lines. Keep them soft, breaking them in places.

CHEEKS: THE STENCIL PAINT METHOD

This is done after the rest of your project has been painted and allowed to dry. Make sure all transfer lines are erased.

Using a palette knife, peel away a small part of the skin from the Calico Red stencil paint, pick up a touch of paint and place on your palette. With a cotton swab, pick up a little of the paint and apply to the cheeks by using a circular motion or by just dabbing it. Smooth out edges with the clean end of the swab.

Because the stencil paint contains oil, it takes quite a while to dry. It is helpful to spray the cheeks with Krylon #1311 Matte Finish Spray Coating before adding the highlights (this will help the paint dry more quickly) or let dry. If you highlight without the spray, you are taking a chance of rubbing off some of the paint.

STEPS (AND BRUSH POSITION) FOR SHADING FACES

Please refer to the faces on the Colour Worksheets.

FULL FACES

1. *Around the face:* colour side is toward outside edge.

2. *Across the face:* colour side is down. Starting from the side, at the hairline and at the level of the eye, curve up and along the crease of the eyelid, down to and across the narrowest part of the bridge of the nose*, up above and along the other eyelid crease, down to level of the corner of the eye, curve up slightly, and then end at the other hairline. Use the clean corner of the brush to blend the harsh line across the bridge of the nose.

   NOTE: You may need to walk the brush up a bit (between the eyes) to widen the shading.

3. Add small "C"-shaped floats on both sides of the bridge of the nose, at the corners of the eyes. Colour side is toward the bridge of the nose.

4. *Top of the cheeks:* colour side is up.

5. *Top of the nose:* colour side is down; use a small, soft stroke. This is mostly for young faces.

6. *Underneath the bottom lip:* colour side is down.

7. *Cheeks:* colour side is toward the mouth. The rounded float starts at the flare of the nostril; leave a small space

(Continued on Page 8)

Painting Faces and Bodies
(Continued from Page 7)

between the nostril and the shading. Sometimes I use a colour-to-colour float to shade under the cheek, forming a triangle between the two floats and then blending it softly. When you do the first rounded float, bring it under the cheek, then flip the brush over and pull another float overlapping the colour, widening the second float as you work towards the side of the face. Repeat until nicely blended.

8. *Nose:* colour side is toward the outside edge of the flare of the nose. Use tiny "C" strokes, blended only once or twice on the palette. First left flare, left centre. Bring the centre shading into a shallow "v" at the lower part of nose. Shade the right flare and right centre.

9. Add a small, narrow "U" shape between the nose and the mouth (if shown on the design). Start with the brush upright, colour side facing six o'clock. Then just paint a small "U" without changing the position of the brush.

10. On larger faces I sometimes add a colour-to-colour float on one side of the nose. Float down from the hollow (beside the bridge of the nose) toward the shading indicating the tip of the nose. Flip the brush over and float again, overlapping the floats. Repeat until nicely blended.

11. If the ears are showing, shade next to the face first. Colour side is toward the face. Then shade around the edges of the ear, ear lobe and the inner detail.

12. Shade all around the neck, and add extra shading under the chin.

TURNED FACE
Add shading along the nose and mouth on the narrow side of the face. Colour side is toward the nose.

SIDE VIEW
Follow the steps as described for the full face, with the following exceptions:

1. Step 1 is the same. The shading in front is very light and soft. (It only softens the outline a bit.)

2. Start floating from the front of the eyebrow, with colour side toward the front of the face. Then bring it down to and along the crease of the eyelid. Pull away and end before the hairline.

3. Shade in front of the eye with a small "C" stroke, colour toward the eye.

   Leave out steps 4, 5 and 6.

4. The rounded float starts from the top of the cheek, a little below the eye. Colour is toward the mouth.

5. Shade only the flare of the nose.

   Leave out steps 9 and 10.

6. Same as steps 11 and 12.

Little Apple Fairy
Tray, Apple Box and Teakettle
Photo on Front Cover; Worksheet on Page 9; Patterns on Pages 9-11

PALETTE
DELTA CERAMCOAT ACRYLICS
Bambi Brown
Black Green
Dark Forest Green
Fleshtone
Light Ivory
Old Parchment
Sandstone
Stonewedge Green
Tomato Spice
Walnut
DELTA CERAMCOAT GLEAMS
14K Gold
DECOART EASY BLEND STENCIL PAINT
Calico Red

BRUSHES
Jackie Shaw Liner: #2
Liner: #2/0 or smaller
Round Scumbler: 1/2" or smaller
Shader: #4, #8 and #12
Wash/Glaze: 3/4"

OTHER SUPPLIES
Delta Ceramcoat Artist Gesso (if needed)
Delta Ceramcoat Sparkle Glaze
Plastic cling wrap

BACKGROUND PREPARATION
TRAY: *NOTE: The middle areas of the trays may vary in size. Adjust pattern size to fit.* Seal tray, sand, and remove sanding dust. If the surface is rough, try applying gesso for a smoother painting surface. Basecoat the centre with Sandstone, and the rim with Stonewedge Green.

Have two pieces of crumpled plastic wrap ready. Using the 3/4" wash brush (or 1" foam brush), quickly apply thinned Dark Forest Green on the rim. Dab the wet surface with one of the pieces of plastic wrap. Let dry and repeat with thinned Sandstone. This time, try to get nice, even texture. (I confess to wiping this last application off a couple of times before it was satisfactory.)

If necessary, paint the outer edge of the centre of the tray again with Sandstone. Let dry well.

(Continued on Page 10)

Little Apple Fairy

Little Apple Fairy

Teakettle Motif

Reverse design for opposite side

Little Apple Fairy
(Continued from Page 8)

APPLE BOX AND TEAKETTLE: Follow instructions for the tray. Seal and sand the box, but the papier-mâché kettle does not need preparation.

Refer to the colour photo for placement of stippled trim. Apply the stippled trim before basecoating the design area with Sandstone. When dry, use low-tack masking tape to mask off the stippled edges of the box when basecoating the lighter areas. The dark green trim along bottom of box and kettle, the box handle and knob on kettle lid are painted with Dark Forest Green.

Transfer main pattern lines.

PAINTING PROCEDURE

Tray

Basecoat skin areas with Fleshtone; while waiting to dry, proceed with the following components of the design.

APPLES

Basecoat with Old Parchment. Using the #12 flat brush, float shading on the lighter sides and the front edge of the blossom and stem ends (where stems attach to apples) with Stonewedge Green. Float shading on darker sides and inside indentations of the stem ends with Dark Forest Green. Float shading inside the indentations of blossom ends, first with Tomato Spice and then with a touch of Dark Forest Green.

Using the 3/4" wash brush for larger apples and the #12 flat brush for smaller ones, gradually shade and build up colour by floating Tomato Spice. "Walk" the brush to widen shading. Let dry between coats. With the dirty brush, pick up some Old Parchment on the red corner, then blend on the palette. With the chisel edge of the brush, colour side down, pull stripes up from the bottom of the dark half of apple. Let the stripes fade before reaching the top. The largest apple in the front is the brightest.

To darken the shading, first sideload the brush with Tomato Spice, then add a touch of Black Green to the same corner. Blend on the palette and apply.

Drybrush soft highlights with Light Ivory, using a scumbler. Using a liner, add more definite highlights in the centre of the drybrushed highlight.

Add a soft highlight on some of the blossom ends with Stonewedge Green. Use a liner brush and Black Green to paint the dark strokes in the blossom ends.

NOTE: When doing the companion projects, I discovered that it's almost impossible to get the apples looking the same as the originals. It's not at all important. Just work with them until they look good enough to eat!

LEAVES

Use a #8 flat brush for the smaller leaves and a #12 for larger ones. Doubleload the brush with Stonewedge Green and Dark Forest Green. Start at the base of each leaf and wiggle your brush back and forth as you pull brush toward the tip (the dark colour is toward the centre). Repeat for the other side (light colour is toward the centre).

Doubleload the #4 flat or round with Dark Forest Green and Old Parchment to paint the turned areas of the leaves.

Float shading with Dark Forest Green behind overlapping apples or leaves. Tint leaves with Tomato Spice. Float Old Parchment highlights along edges of light sides of leaves.

Little Apple Fairy
Tray

BRANCHES AND STEMS

Basecoat branches with Bambi Brown. Use the #2 liner with Walnut for shading and detail.

Add leaf and apple stems with Stonewedge Green. Using the liner, shade stems first with strokes of Dark Forest Green and then with a touch of Black Green.

FAIRY

WINGS: With the kneaded eraser, erase the transfer lines until only slightly visible.

Using the 3/4" wash brush, float edges of the three wing sections with Old Parchment. With the sideloaded brush and Old Parchment, fill in the wing sections, starting at the back of the fairy and walking the brush toward the centre of the wings.

(Continued on Page 12)

Box Motifs

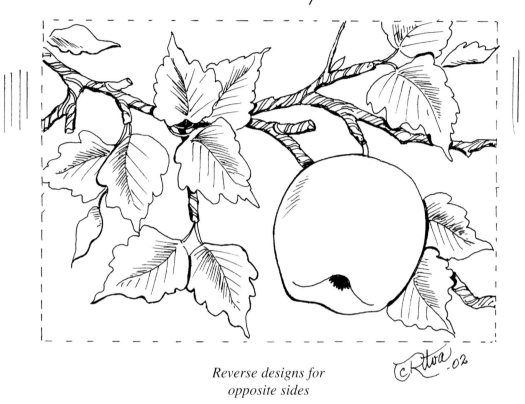

*Reverse designs for
opposite sides*

12

Little Apple Fairy
(Continued from Page 11)

Add some Tomato Spice to the yellow corner of the brush, blend on the palette, then float on wing tips; walk the brush to widen. Repeat until satisfactory.

Using the scumbler or a small stippler, lightly stipple Stonewedge Green on the lower wing section. Float shading on the back wing (behind front wing) and behind the fairy with very thin Black Green.

The veins are painted with very fine lines of Black Green. Add small dots of Black Green. Using a liner brush, add Light Ivory highlights on top edge of each small wing section.

FACE AND BODY: Please refer to "Painting Faces and Bodies."

Transfer details, including outlines. Touch up any skin areas with the basecoat colour as needed. Set detail and outline with very fine lines of Bambi Brown. When dry, erase transfer lines.

Float shading with Bambi Brown. Float Tomato Spice on all shading. Brush-mix Old Parchment + a touch of Tomato Spice, then paint the lips. Highlight bottom lip with Light Ivory.

Using a small liner brush and thinned Walnut, darken eyebrows with fine lines (in growth direction), darken the outline where necessary for definition and add tiny nostrils. Use Black Green to paint lashes and centre mouth line. Add small highlights to his right arm and thighs with Light Ivory.

Do the cheeks *last*, after the rest of the painting has been completed, with the stencil paint method. Make sure all transfer lines are erased first. The stencil paint may also be added on the chin and wherever it may be needed. Allow the paint to dry (or spray with Krylon #1311), then add a small Light Ivory highlight on the cheek.

HAIR: Basecoat with Old Parchment. Shade with fine, uneven lines of Bambi Brown and darken with thinned Walnut. Highlight with touches of Light Ivory.

SUIT: Basecoat with Stonewedge Green. Float shading and add details with Dark Forest Green. Float highlights with Old Parchment.

GRASS
Basecoat grass area with a thin wash of Dark Forest Green. Add blades of grass with Dark Forest Green. Float shading under apple and fairy's feet with Dark Forest Green.

FINISHING TOUCHES
Apply sparkle glaze to the wings. Paint lines of Dark Forest Green and 14K Gold around the centre using the "carpenter's trick" (refer to the "General Instructions").

Apple Box and Teakettle

Paint the apples, leaves, branches, stems and grass following the instructions for the tray.

Paint the lines with Dark Forest Green and 14K Gold, referring to the colour photograph for placement.

FINISH AND ENJOY!

Blueberry Fairy
Plate and Hurricane Lamp
Photo on Page 14; Worksheet on Page 15; Patterns on Pages 12-13 & 16

PALETTE
DELTA CERAMCOAT ACRYLICS
Bambi Brown
Blue Velvet
Butter Cream
Candy Bar Brown (Lamp)
Dark Foliage Green (Lamp)
Fleshtone
Light Foliage Green
Light Ivory
Medium Foliage Green
Old Parchment (Lamp)
Pine Green
Purple Dusk
Rouge (Lamp)
Royal Plum
Sea Grass
Tomato Spice
Walnut
DECOART EASY BLEND STENCIL PAINT
Calico Red

BRUSHES
Deerfoot Stippler: 1/8"
Jackie Shaw Liner: #2
Liner: #2/0 or smaller
Shader: #4, #8 and #12
Wash/Glaze: 3/4"

BACKGROUND PREPARATION
Please refer to the "General Instructions" for background preparation.

(Continued on Page 16)

Blueberry Fairy

Plate

14

Blueberry Fairy
Pages 12-13 & 16-17

Wild Strawberry Fairy
Pages 17-19

Wild Strawberry Fairy

15

1

2

Lace Detail

1

2

3

4

Blueberry Fairy

1

2

3

4

Ritva -02

Ritva -02

Blueberry Fairy
(Continued from Page 12)

PLATE: Basecoat the centre of the plate with Butter Cream and the rim with Blue Velvet until opaque. Let dry thoroughly.

LAMP: Basecoat first with Butter Cream, then mark and paint the borders with Blue Velvet. Let dry thoroughly.

Transfer main pattern lines.

PAINTING PROCEDURE

Plate

BRANCH

Basecoat with Bambi Brown. Lines and shading are Walnut.

Stipple moss first with Pine Green, then with Sea Grass and, lastly, with Light Foliage Green, leaving some of previous stipple colours showing on the edges.

FAIRY

WINGS: Float edges of wing sections with Purple Dusk. Add vein lines with very thin Blue Velvet. Center strokes are Royal Plum.

CLOTHES: Basecoat shirt and hat with Purple Dusk. Add stripes of Tomato Spice, Sea Grass and Light Foliage Green. Float shading on shirt and hat first with Royal Plum, then with Blue Velvet. Highlight with Sea Grass.

For leaves on hat, follow instructions for light leaves.

Basecoat sleeve, pants and slippers with Sea Grass. Lightly float shading with Pine Green. Tint the shaded areas on sleeve and pants with thinned Tomato Spice. Highlight sleeve and pants with Butter Cream. Float Tomato Spice on top edges and tips of slippers.

FACE, NECK AND HANDS: Please refer to "Painting Faces and Bodies."

Blueberry Fairy

Hurricane Lamp
Base Motif

Repeat the pattern on all four sides

Blue Velvet border goes up to the top

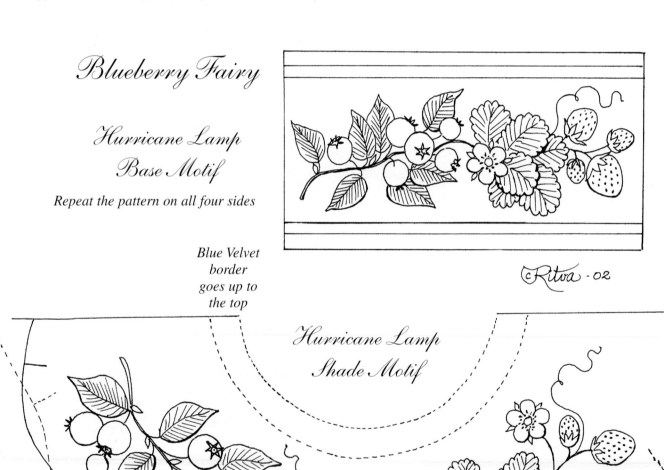

Hurricane Lamp
Shade Motif

Repeat pattern on other side. Mark and line up notches of wavy border line.

Basecoat with Fleshtone. Let dry thoroughly. Transfer detail. Set detail with very thin Bambi Brown. When dry, erase transfer lines.

Float shading with Bambi Brown. Lightly float Tomato Spice on all shading. Lips are painted with thinned Tomato Spice. Add a tiny Light Ivory highlight on lower lip. Inside the mouth is Walnut. Paint tiny indications of teeth with Butter Cream.

Eyes are Blue Velvet. Add highlight dots with Butter Cream.

Use the small liner brush and thinned Walnut to paint hair, eyebrows (tiny strokes in growth direction), other face details and a very fine outline on lower part of the face and hand.

Do the cheeks *last* with the stencil paint method. Make sure all the transfer lines are erased. Allow the paint to dry (or spray with Krylon #1311), then add small Butter Cream highlights on the cheeks.

LEAVES AND STEMS

LIGHT LEAVES: Basecoat with Light Foliage Green. Float shading with Medium Foliage Green. Veins are painted with Sea Grass.

DARK LEAVES: Basecoat with Medium Foliage Green. Float shading with Pine Green. Veins are painted with Light Foliage Green.

STEMS: Basecoat with Medium Foliage Green. Darken where needed with Pine Green. Add little buds with Bambi Brown and then shade the base of each bud with a small stroke of Walnut.

RIM: Leaves on the rim are painted the same as dark leaves. Tendrils and line border are Medium Foliage Green.

BERRIES

RIPE BERRIES: Basecoat with Purple Dusk. Float shading first with Royal Plum and then with Blue Velvet. Float highlight with thinned Sea Grass. For the four "semi-ripe" berries that have a slight reddish cast, drybrush a mix of Light Ivory + Royal Plum in the centre.

Basecoat blossom ends with Royal Plum. Outline where needed with touches of Purple Dusk. Use Sea Grass to paint the centre detail.

RAW BERRIES: Basecoat with Sea Grass. Float shading with Medium Foliage Green. Use a liner and Tomato Spice to paint the blossom ends.

Hurricane Lamp

BERRIES AND BLOSSOMS

Follow instructions for berries and leaves on the "Blueberry Fairy" plate, and for berries, blossoms and leaves on the "Wild Strawberry Fairy" plate. Use the instructions for the light and medium strawberry leaves, but use Pine Green instead of Dark Foliage Green for shading the darker leaves. Paint the stems and tendrils Medium Foliage Green.

The linework and comma strokes on borders are painted with Medium Foliage Green.

FINISH AND ENJOY!

Wild Strawberry Fairy

Photo on Page 14; Worksheet on Page 15; Pattern on Pages 18-19

PALETTE
DELTA CERAMCOAT ACRYLICS
Bambi Brown
Blue Velvet
Candy Bar Brown
Dark Foliage Green
Fleshtone
Light Foliage Green
Light Ivory
Medium Foliage Green
Old Parchment
Rouge
Soft Grey
DECOART EASY BLEND STENCIL PAINT
Calico Red

BRUSHES
Jackie Shaw Liner: #2
Liner: #2/0 or smaller
Round: #0 or #1
Shader: #8 and #12
Wash/Glaze: 3/4"

BACKGROUND PREPARATION

Please refer to the "General Instructions" for background preparation.

Basecoat the centre of the plate with Blue Velvet and the rim with Soft Grey until opaque. Let dry thoroughly.

Transfer pattern, leaving out blossoms and berries that overlap underlying areas that need to be painted first.

PAINTING PROCEDURE
FAIRY

NOTE: Refer to instructions for painting light leaves. Paint the leaf behind the wing before painting wings.

WINGS: Float outer edges of wing sections with Soft Grey. Repeat until satisfactory. Using the chisel edge of a sideloaded flat brush, pull Soft Grey stripes, starting from the outer edge.

Float the middle shapes with Old Parchment and float the inner shapes with Rouge.

Using Rouge, float around the outside of the yellow shapes, and pull a few stripes upward, using the same method as on edges of wings.

(Continued on Page 18)

Wild Strawberry Fairy
(Continued from Page 17)

FACE AND BODY: Please refer to "Painting Faces and Bodies."

Basecoat with Fleshtone. Let dry thoroughly and then transfer detail. Set detail with very thin Bambi Brown. When dry, erase transfer lines.

Float shading with Bambi Brown. Lightly float Rouge on all shading.

Lips are painted with thinned Rouge. Add a tiny Light Ivory highlight on lower lip. The inside of the mouth is Blue Velvet with a touch of Candy Bar Brown in the middle. Paint tiny indications of teeth with Light Ivory.

Use a liner brush to paint the eyes. Dab a touch of Light Ivory on the centre of the triangles of the "whites" of the eyes. Basecoat the irises with a mix of Light Ivory + a touch of Blue Velvet (for a medium blue colour). Add more Light Ivory to the dirty brush, then lighten each iris, below the pupil.

Paint the pupils with Blue Velvet. Use Blue Velvet to darken upper lashes and corners of the eyes. Add highlight dots to the pupils with Light Ivory.

Using a small liner brush, paint eyebrows (tiny strokes in growth direction), nostrils, corners of the mouth, and arm and leg detail with thinned Candy Bar Brown.

Do the cheeks *last* with the stencil paint method. Make sure all the transfer lines are erased. Allow the paint to dry (or spray with Krylon #1311), then add small Light Ivory highlights on the cheeks.

HAIR: Basecoat with Bambi Brown. Shade with fine strokes of very thin Candy Bar Brown. Add highlights with strokes of Old Parchment. The little ribbons are painted with Rouge.

SUIT: Basecoat with Medium Foliage Green. Float shading with Dark Foliage Green. Float highlights with Old Parchment. Using Light Ivory, paint the lace trim around armholes and legs. The petal collar and hat are painted in the same manner as the blossoms.

LEAVES AND STEMS

Basecoat leaves with liner strokes, starting at the edges and pulling toward the centre vein. Repeat until opaque.

LIGHT LEAVES: Basecoat with Light Foliage Green. Float shading along centre vein line, and under overlapping berries, blossoms and stems with Medium Foliage Green. Veins are painted with thinned Medium Foliage Green. Using the #2 liner, highlight with touches of Old Parchment. Wipe the brush on a paper towel to remove excess paint before highlighting.

DARK LEAVES (in centre): Basecoat with Dark Foliage Green. Highlight lightly with Medium Foliage Green.

MEDIUM LEAVES (on rim): Basecoat with Medium Foliage Green. Use Dark Foliage Green to float shading on leaves and to paint veins.

STEMS: In the centre section, stems and tendrils are painted with Light Foliage Green. Darken and outline stems where needed with Medium Foliage Green or Dark Foliage Green.

On the rim, the stems and tendrils are Medium Foliage Green.

BERRIES

Transfer berries and blossoms.

RIPE BERRIES: Basecoat with Rouge. Lightly float Light Ivory to highlight. Float shading (just in from outer edge) and paint dots with Candy Bar Brown. Using a liner, add brighter highlights between seeds with dots of Light Ivory. On the berries in the centre section only, add a touch of Old Parchment in some of the dark dots to indicate seeds.

RAW BERRIES: Basecoat with Old Parchment. Float shading and paint dots with Medium Foliage Green. Float highlight with Light Ivory. Lightly float Rouge on some of the raw berries.

BLOSSOMS

Basecoat with Light Ivory. Float Blue Velvet shading around the centres. Centres are painted with Old Parchment. Add stamens using a mix of Old Parchment + a touch of Rouge.

FINISHING TOUCHES

Add calyxes and flick leaves using Medium Foliage Green on the rim and Light Foliage Green in the centre. (I have darkened some of the blossom sepals that overlap the light leaves with Dark Foliage Green.)

Stroke in some blades of grass with Dark Foliage Green and then stroke a few with Medium Foliage Green.

FINISH AND ENJOY!

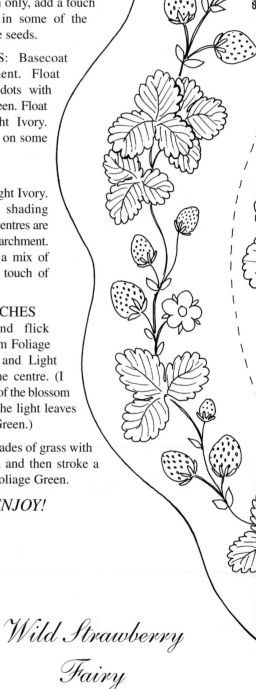

Wild Strawberry Fairy

Blue Fairies

Pages 22-24

Blue Fairies

Before adding colour on hair, shade first with Nightfall Blue

Blue Fairies

Photo on Page 20; Worksheet on Page 21; Patterns on Pages 22-23

PALETTE
DELTA CERAMCOAT ACRYLICS
Antique Gold
Drizzle Grey
Medium Foliage Green
Nightfall Blue
Rouge
Soft Grey
Spice Brown

BRUSHES
Jackie Shaw Liner: #1 or #2
Liner: #2/0 or smaller
Shader: #10 or #12

OTHER SUPPLIES
Delta Ceramcoat Sparkle Glaze

BACKGROUND PREPARATION

Please refer to the "General Instructions" for preparation information. Basecoat the plates with Drizzle Grey. Let dry thoroughly.

Transfer the whole pattern, leaving out only the dots and details that you can do freehand. If your lines are too dark, use a kneaded eraser to lighten them before proceeding.

Set all the transferred lines with fine, *very* thin lines of Nightfall Blue. When dry, erase all transfer lines completely.

METHOD

Except for the liner work, all colour is floated with a flat brush. Use paint very sparingly for sheer applications. Load the brush by picking up paint on just a few hairs of one corner. Practice first.

EVERYTHING, including faces and skin, is painted and shaded first with Nightfall Blue. Other colours will be applied later.

(Continued on Page 24)

Blue Fairies

Blue Fairies
(Continued from Page 23)

NOTE: The techniques used for these pieces are floating and using thin, watercolour-like washes that do not hide what's underneath. Therefore, it is important that transfer lines do not show, and that components are painted separately and allowed to dry before painting overlapping components.

PAINTING PROCEDURE
FAIRIES

FACES AND BODIES: Please refer to the shading faces section under "Painting Faces and Bodies." Follow only the positioning for shading, ignoring the instructions for basecoat and shading colours.

Float shading on the skin with thinned Nightfall Blue. Also use thinned Nightfall Blue to delicately darken outlines and details. Do not paint harsh lines.

Float Rouge on all skin areas. Float the cheeks a bit brighter than rest of blushing, by either adding more colour to the first application or by floating a second time. Float a soft highlight on the cheeks with Soft Grey.

Lips are painted with thinned Rouge, with Soft Grey highlights on lower lips. Irises are Nightfall Blue. Add a Soft Grey highlight dot to the iris of the fairy looking up. Float Soft Grey highlights on the shoulder and hand of the fairy looking down.

HAIR: Float shading with Nightfall Blue. Apply a wash using Spice Brown. Highlight with Soft Grey, either by floating, stroking or applying a combination of the two.

WINGS: Float shading with Nightfall Blue. Use appropriate size brush handle and Nightfall Blue for dots on wings. Float tints of Antique Gold and Rouge where indicated on the worksheet. Float highlights with Soft Grey.

DRESSES: Float shading with Nightfall Blue. Float highlights with Soft Grey.

FLOWERS AND LEAVES

Use a sideloaded brush to paint stroke leaves, flower petals and buds with Nightfall Blue. The open flowers have little Nightfall Blue lines radiating from the centres. Use the chisel edge of the sideloaded flat brush to paint them or, if you prefer, use a liner.

Float Medium Foliage Green on leaves; add touches of Antique Gold to some of them. Using Nightfall Blue, darken stems, paint veins on leaves, and add flick leaves and calyxes. Using a liner, highlight leaves with Soft Grey. Float Rouge and/or Antique Gold on flowers and buds in varying amounts. Float centres of open flowers with Antique Gold + a touch of Spice Brown. When dry, add some tiny Nightfall Blue dots to shaded areas of centres. Add highlights and stylus dots with Soft Grey.

FINISHING TOUCHES

Float a soft tint of Antique Gold around the fairies. Add Sparkle Glaze to the wings.

FINISH AND ENJOY!

Baking Fairies
Breadboard, Recipe Box and Note Holder
Photo on Page 29; Worksheet on Page 28; Patterns on Pages 25-27

Breadboard

PALETTE
DELTA CERAMCOAT ACRYLICS
Bambi Brown
Blue Haze
Flesh Tan
Fleshtone
Light Ivory
Spice Brown
Terra Cotta
Walnut
DECOART EASY BLEND STENCIL PAINT
Calico Red

BRUSHES
Jackie Shaw Liner: #1 or #2
Liner: #2/0 or smaller
Shader: #2, #8 and #12
Wash/Glaze: 3/4"

OTHER SUPPLIES
Clapham's Beeswax Salad Bowl Finish (if breadboard is to be used for food)
Delta Ceramcoat Gel Stain Medium
Low-tack masking tape

BACKGROUND PREPARATION

Mix Spice Brown + Gel Stain Medium (1:2). Using a damp cloth, apply stain on both sides of board. Let dry. Using a #12 flat brush, apply very thin, vertical streaks of Terra Cotta and Blue Haze on the centre area. Let dry. Spray with one coat of Krylon #1311.

Using the 3/4" wash brush, float shading around the inner edge of centre area with Walnut.

Thinly wash the table top, under the bread, with Spice Brown. Pull a few horizontal lines with thinned Walnut to indicate wood texture.

Transfer only the breads, ignoring the fairies.

PAINTING PROCEDURE
BREADS

Basecoat with Flesh Tan until opaque. Try to avoid ridges along top edges. Let dry.

Using the #12 flat brush, float shading with Spice Brown. It may help to dampen surface first. Begin by floating across the middle of loaf. Then, float across the top of loaf and work downward, "walking" the brush to extend the shading. Remember, these are "baked goods"—they do not need to be perfectly even. Also shade the loaf around the bun. Shade the bun and establish the cross in the middle. Darken the deepest shading with Walnut, if necessary.

When the breads are dark enough, apply a thin wash of Terra Cotta on the shading to add a bit of colour. Float highlights with Light Ivory.

Seeds are little ovals of Flesh Tan. Use a liner to shade with Spice Brown and highlight with dabs of Light Ivory.

Float shading on the table under the breads with Walnut.

When dry, transfer rest of pattern, leaving out detail on faces, clothing and the wings of centre figure. Float shading on the bread, around fairies, with Spice Brown.

FAIRIES

FACES, HANDS AND HAIR: Please refer to "Painting Faces and Bodies."

Basecoat faces and hands with Fleshtone. Let dry thoroughly and then transfer skin details.

Set (establish) details and outline faces with very fine lines of Bambi Brown. At this point, only thinly dot the eyebrows. When dry, erase transfer lines.

Float shading on skin areas with Bambi Brown. Float very thin Terra Cotta on all shading.

Lips are painted with thin Terra Cotta. Add highlight on lower lip with Light Ivory.

Using a small liner brush and Walnut, darken eyebrows with tiny, fine lines (in growth direction), paint the eyes, add wisps of hair and define the outlines. Darken other details, such as nostrils, mouth line, etc., also with Walnut. Highlight eyes with a dot of Light Ivory. Use the liner brush to stroke in the hair with Walnut.

Paint the cheeks *last*, after rest of the painting has been completed, with the stencil paint method. Make sure all transfer lines are erased first. The stencil paint may also be added to the chin and wherever it may be needed. Allow the paint to dry (or spray with Krylon #1311), then add small Light Ivory highlights to the cheeks, nose and bottom lip.

CLOTHES: Basecoat hats and shirts with Light Ivory. Float shading with Blue Haze.

Basecoat pants with Terra Cotta. Float shading first with Spice Brown and then darken with Walnut. Pants are highlighted with Flesh Tan.

Shoes are basecoated with Spice Brown and shaded with Walnut. Liner detail is also Walnut.

WINGS: Transfer the wings of middle fairy.

Starting with the back wings, float outer edges of all wing sections with Blue Haze. When dry, float the front wings of the side fairies again, this time with Light Ivory. Float Light Ivory along both wings of the middle fairy, leaving some of the blue showing on the edges of wings. Float the inner shapes with Flesh Tan.

Using a small liner, pull a few thin lines on each wing section with Terra Cotta, radiating outward from the back. To separate the middle fairy's wings, touch up the centre with Light Ivory. Add stylus dots with Walnut.

(Continued on Page 26)

Baking Fairies

Note Holder Motifs

Baking Fairies
(Continued from Page 25)

FINISHING TOUCHES

Brush some Flesh Tan on the wheat on the rim and use Flesh Tan to pull lines on raised parts of the tips. Add a dab of Light Ivory to highlight each kernel.

Paint the outer edge of the board with Blue Haze.

If you wish to use a beeswax finish, follow the manufacturer's instructions for application.

Recipe Box and Note Holder

BACKGROUND PREPARATION

Seal both pieces with one coat of Delta Ceramcoat All-Purpose Sealer BEFORE applying the stain. These surfaces were so much more porous than the plate that I found it necessary to seal first. Let dry and sand with fine sandpaper. Apply the stain.

On the note holder, transfer the pattern line for the centre circle. To mask off the area around the circle, first draw the circle on a piece of paper. Then cut out the circle, and trim the paper to fit the front panel. Secure the paper with tape. When streaking, try to avoid getting paint under the paper.

On the front of the recipe box, transfer pattern line for centre shape. Use tape to mask around the centre shape.

Follow the breadboard instructions for streaking the centre areas. After streaking, remove the paper from the note holder and the tape from the recipe box. Seal again with sealer and let dry.

Transfer only the patterns for the breads.

Recipe Box Motif

PAINTING PROCEDURE

Paint a line around the centre shapes with Walnut. Float around the inside edges of the shapes with Walnut.

Paint the edges, buns and fairies in the same manner as on the breadboard. The bows are Blue Haze.

Basecoat the wheat and shafts with strokes of Flesh Tan. Float shading on each kernel with Spice Brown and then high-light with a dot of Light Ivory. Using Spice Brown, outline the kernels with fine lines and outline one side of each shaft. Add the fine lines coming from the top and sides of wheat with Flesh Tan. (I tried to find out what those things on the ends of the wheat kernels are called, with no luck!)

FINISH AND ENJOY!

Baking Fairies

Breadboard Motif

Colour Swatches

These colour swatches represent all the colours used in this book. I have included them for your reference in case you need to mix or make substitutions.

- Antique Gold
- Bambi Brown
- Barn Red
- Black Green
- Blue Haze
- Blue Velvet
- Butter Cream
- Candy Bar Brown
- Chocolate Cherry
- Dark Foliage Green
- Dark Forest Green
- Drizzle Grey
- Eggshell White
- Flesh Tan
- Fleshtone
- Lavender Lace
- Light Foliage Green
- Light Ivory
- Medium Foliage Green
- Nightfall Blue
- Old Parchment
- Palomino Tan
- Pine Green
- Purple Dusk
- Rouge
- Royal Plum
- Sandstone
- Sea Grass
- Soft Grey
- Spice Brown
- Stonewedge Green
- Straw
- Terra Cotta
- Tomato Spice
- Walnut
- 14K Gold (Gleams)

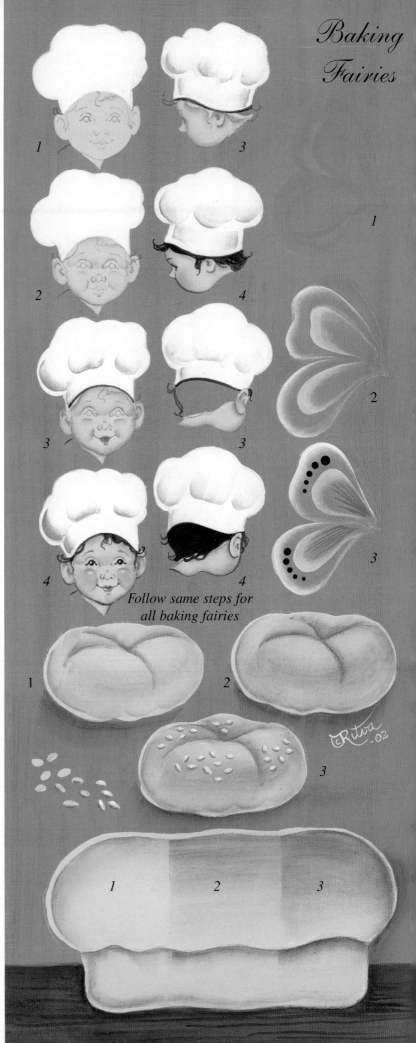

Baking Fairies

Follow same steps for all baking fairies

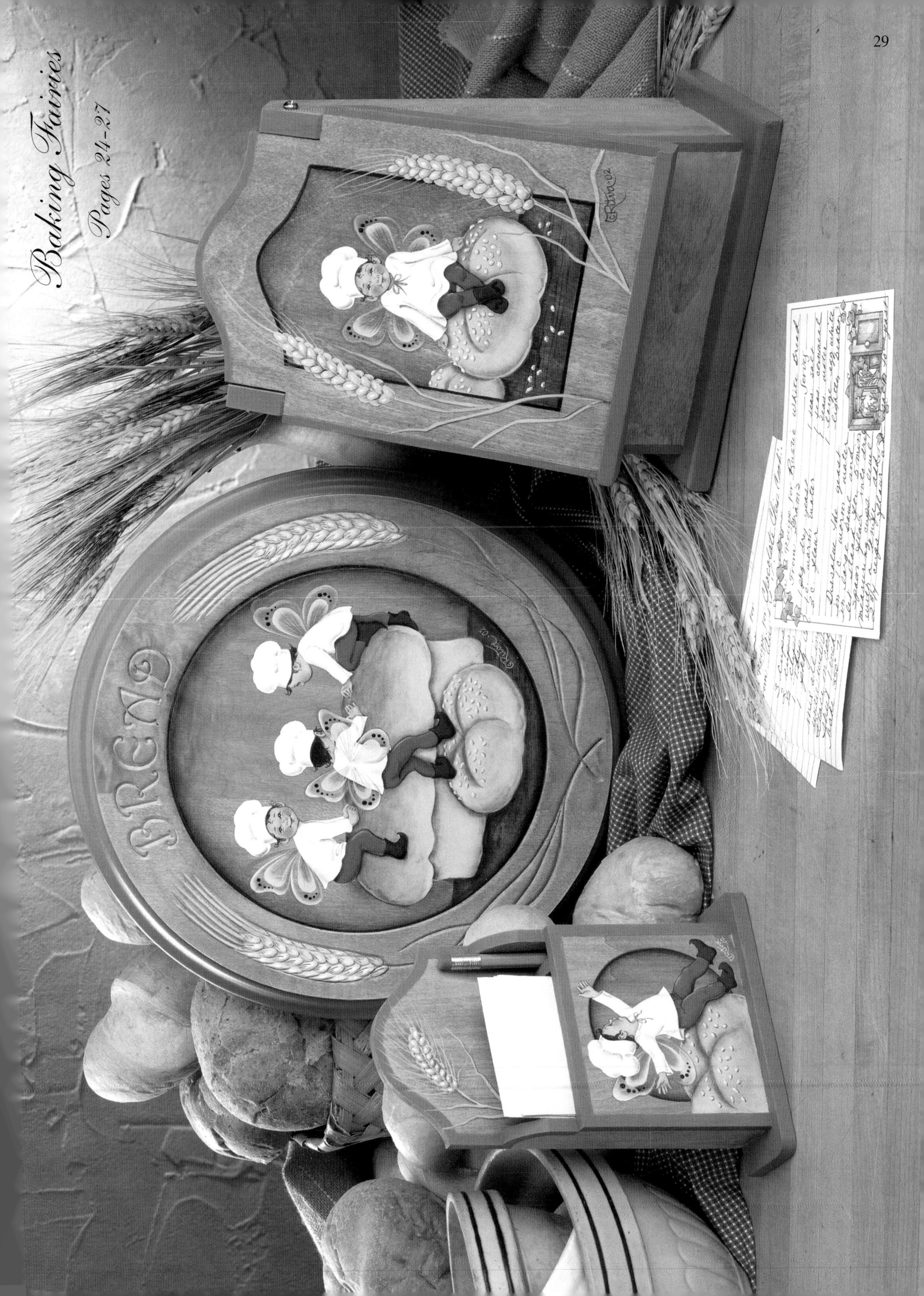

Baking Fairies

Pages 24-27

Poppy Fairy
Plate and Water Pitcher
Photo on Page 32; Worksheet on Page 33; Patterns on Pages 30-31 & 34

PALETTE
DELTA CERAMCOAT ACRYLICS
Bambi Brown
Black Green
Dark Foliage Green
Eggshell White
Fleshtone
Lavender Lace
Light Foliage Green
Medium Foliage Green
Straw
Tomato Spice
DELTA CERAMCOAT GLEAMS
14K Gold
DECOART EASY BLEND STENCIL PAINT
Calico Red

BRUSHES
Jackie Shaw Liner: #2
Liner: #2/0 or smaller
Shader: #8 and #12
Wash/Glaze: 3/4"

OTHER SUPPLIES
Loew-Cornell Fine Line Painting Pen (optional)

Plate

BACKGROUND PREPARATION
Please refer to wood preparation in the "General Instructions." Basecoat with Eggshell White. When dry, mark the border 3/4" (19 mm) from the outside edge. Basecoat border and back of plate with Black Green. Let dry. Transfer main pattern lines.

PAINTING PROCEDURE
FLOWERS
POPPIES: Basecoat the petals with Straw. Doubleload the 3/4" wash brush with Straw and Tomato Spice. Blend on the palette, then pick up more paint, building up the colour in the brush. There should be quite a bit of paint in the brush to complete a petal. Paint the back petals first. The petals are painted by using ruffled "C" strokes, with the Tomato Spice edge of the brush following along the outside edge of each petal.

Centres of the flowers are Black Green with a cross of Medium Foliage Green. Add the stamen lines and stylus dots with Black Green.

FILLER FLOWERS: The delicate filler-flower clusters are dots of Lavender Lace with a dot of Straw in each individual flower centre. The stems and flick leaves are Light Foliage Green.

FACE AND BODY
Please refer to "Painting Faces and Bodies." Basecoat face, arms and legs with Fleshtone until opaque. Transfer details.

Set outlines and details with very fine lines of Bambi Brown. (Only thinly dot the eyebrows.) When dry, erase transfer lines.

Float shading with Bambi Brown. Float thin Tomato Spice on all shading.

Lips show only narrowly in the front of the face. Use thinned Tomato Spice.

Mix a warm brown using Medium Foliage Green + Tomato Spice. Lightly darken the skin outlines and details here and there. Paint the lashes with Black Green.

Paint the cheeks *last,* after the rest of the painting has been completed, using the stencil paint method. Erase all transfer lines first. The stencil paint may also be added to the chin, arms, legs, and wherever it may be needed. Allow the paint to dry (or spray with Krylon #1311).

HAIR
Basecoat the hair with a mix of Straw + a touch of Tomato Spice. Shade with strokes of the brown mix used to darken skin detail. Also use the brown mix to add a couple of fine, longer lines to indicate direction of hair. Highlight with a few strokes each of Straw and Eggshell White.

FAIRY'S SUIT, LEAVES AND STEMS
LIGHT LEAVES: Basecoat with Light Foliage Green. Float shading with Medium Foliage Green. To highlight, pick up Light Foliage Green on the corner of your clean brush, blend on the palette and then pick up a touch of Eggshell White on the same corner. Blend and apply.

FAIRY SUIT: Follow directions for the light leaves, but darken the shading by also floating with Dark Foliage Green. Add a bit more Eggshell White to the highlight.

DARK LEAVES: Basecoat with Medium Foliage Green. Float shading with Dark Foliage Green. Float highlights with Light Foliage Green.

STEMS AND CALYX: Basecoat with Light Foliage Green. Shade with Dark Foliage Green.

Apply a bit of thinned Medium Foliage Green on the ground around the fairy's feet to indicate grass.

(Continued on Page 35)

Poppy Fairy

Plate Motif

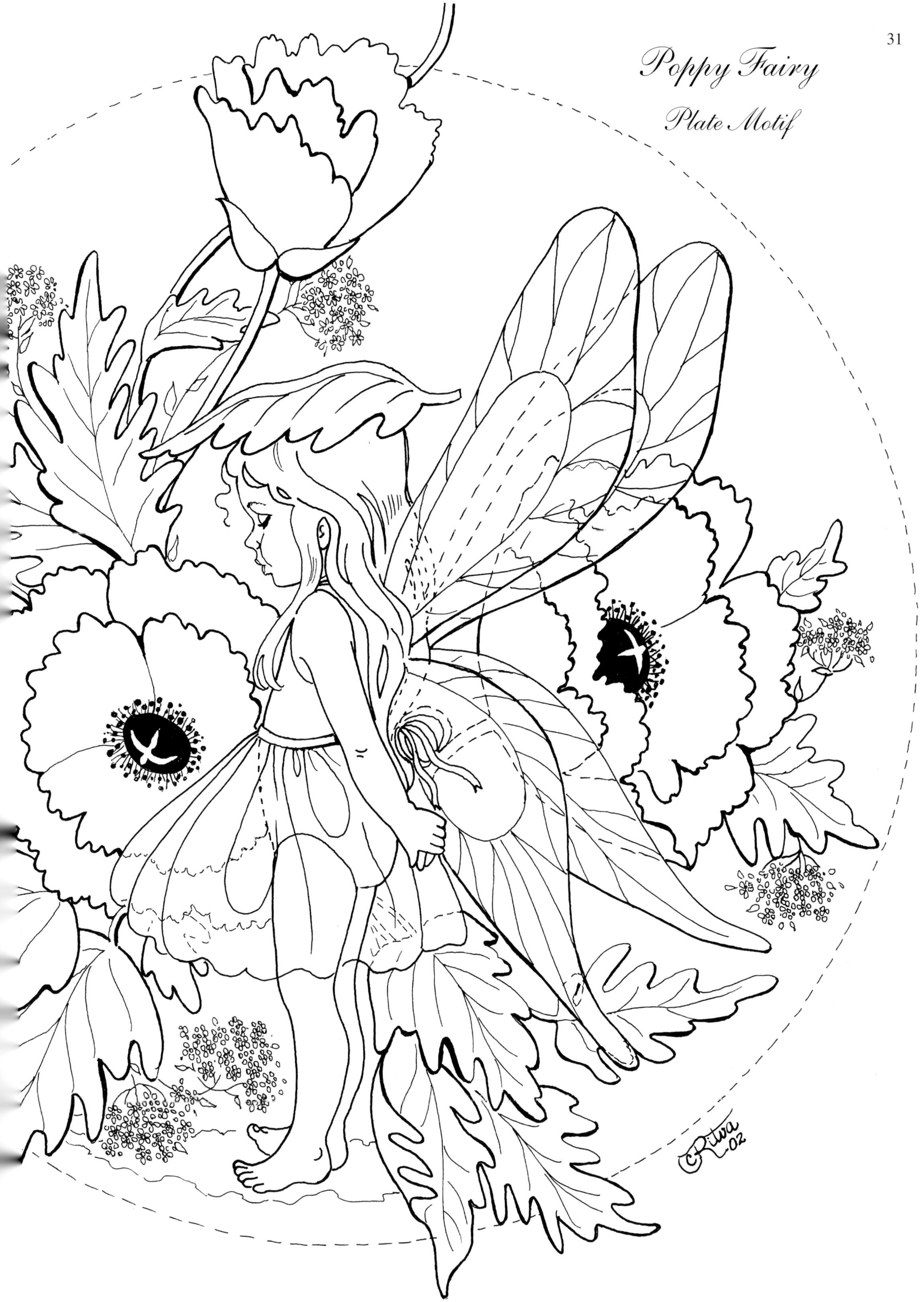

Poppy Fairy

Pages 30-31 & 34-35

Poppy Fairy

Ritva -02

Poppy Fairy
Water Pitcher Motif

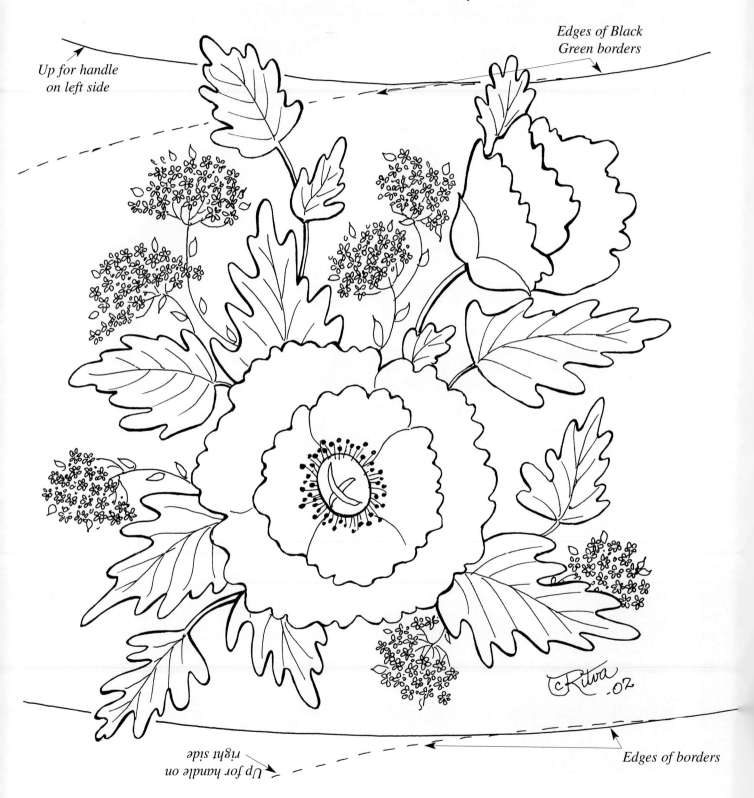

Up for handle
on left side

Edges of Black
Green borders

Up for handle on
right side

Edges of borders

cRitva .02

Poppy Fairy
(Continued from Page 30)
WINGS AND SKIRT

Apply a wash of Lavender Lace over the wings and then float outer edges with more intense colour. The upper edge of the back wing (the area behind the front wing) is done lightly to make the wings look transparent. Note that part of the hair can be seen through the wings.

Using a liner and very thin Black Green, mark the veins of the wings. Apply a thinned Tomato Spice tint to bottom of each section and an Eggshell White highlight to top of each section.

Float the folds of the skirt and the hem with Eggshell White where it overlaps other elements and with Lavender Lace over the background colour.

The ribbon is Tomato Spice with small Eggshell White highlights. Apply a Lavender Lace wash over the ribbon on the wing. Also use Lavender Lace to lighten the stem of the flower showing through the wing.

FINISHING TOUCHES

Mark a line approximately 1/8" (3mm) from the inner edge of the plate rim and another line 1/2" (12mm) from the outer edge. Using a fine liner (or the painting pen) and 14K Gold, paint a narrow stripe over line closer to the centre. Apply an "S"-stroke and stylus dot border on the second line.

Water Pitcher

See instructions for metal preparation in the "General Instructions." For colours and painting, follow instructions for the "Poppy Fairy" plate.

FINISH AND ENJOY!

Celebration!
Plate and Ornaments
Photo on Back Cover; Worksheet on Page 39; Pattern on Pages 36-38

PALETTE
DELTA CERAMCOAT ACRYLICS
Bambi Brown
Barn Red
Blue Velvet
Fleshtone
Light Ivory
Old Parchment
Palomino Tan
Rouge
Walnut
DELTA CERAMCOAT GLEAMS
14K Gold
DECOART EASY BLEND STENCIL PAINT
Calico Red

BRUSHES
Jackie Shaw Liner: #2
Liner: #2/0 or smaller
Round: #4
Shader: #8 and #12
Wash/Glaze: 3/4"

OTHER SUPPLIES
Chalk pencil
Plastic cling wrap

BACKGROUND PREPARATION
Please refer to wood preparation in the "General Instructions." Basecoat the plate and ornaments with Blue Velvet.

PAINTING PROCEDURE
Plate

BACKGROUND
Have a piece of crumpled plastic cling wrap ready. Apply thinned Barn Red on the rim, then stipple with the plastic wrap. Let dry. Using a chalk pencil and the "carpenter's trick" (refer to the "General Instructions") method, mark the rim line. Any areas where the Barn Red stippling has overlapped the plate centre can be cleaned up by applying Blue Velvet again up to the rim line.

Transfer or mark only the arc of the centre "halo" (broken lines on pattern above and behind buildings). Basecoat the inner circle with Palomino Tan and the outer circle with Barn Red. Let dry. Dampen the area. Doubleload the 3/4" wash brush with Palomino Tan and Barn Red. With the tan side of the brush toward the inside, paint around the inner arc for a smooth gradation of colours, covering and hiding the hard line where the colours meet. Repeat until satisfactory. Try to avoid leaving ridges.

Clean the brush and doubleload with Blue Velvet and Barn Red. *NOTE: I used only water in the brush to blend the colors, but you could use blending medium or retarder.* With the blue colour toward the dark background, paint around the outer arc. When the colours are nicely blended, let dry thoroughly.

Transfer only the buildings and the wavy line below them. Basecoat the buildings and area below with Blue Velvet. Add rows of windows to buildings with Palomino Tan.

Transfer main design areas of the pattern.

(Continued on Page 36)

Celebration!
(Continued from Page 35)

ANGELS

FACE AND BODIES: Please refer to "Painting Faces and Bodies." Basecoat with Fleshtone until opaque. Let dry thoroughly. Transfer detail. Set detail with very thin Bambi Brown. When dry, erase transfer lines.

Float shading with Bambi Brown. Lightly float Rouge on all shading.

Lips are painted with thinned Rouge. Add Light Ivory highlights on lower lips where applicable. Eyes are Walnut with a tiny highlight dot of Light Ivory.

Using the small liner brush and thinned Walnut, paint eyebrows (tiny strokes in growth direction); eyelashes; nostrils; and corners, centre lines and inside of the mouths (where applicable). Define other skin details with Bambi Brown and darken some outlines with thinned Walnut.

Do the cheeks *last* with the stencil paint method (again refer to "Painting Faces and Bodies"). Make sure all the transfer lines are erased. Allow the paint to dry (or spray with Krylon #1311), then add small Light Ivory highlights on top of the cheeks. Add some of the stencil paint also on shoulders, elbows or wherever extra blushing is needed.

WINGS AND "COVER-UPS": Paint one wing at a time, starting with those in back.

Outer Feathers: Load the #2 liner with Palomino Tan, sweep from the side of a puddle of Rouge. For every stroke, tip the brush with Light Ivory. Each feather is painted with one stroke.

Smaller Feathers: Do not clean the brush, but wipe excess paint on a paper towel. Tip brush with a touch of Light Ivory for each stroke. Strokes get smaller and smaller toward the angels' backs.

Float shading on the wings next to the angels and to separate the wings with very thin Blue Velvet. Float the scarf-like cover-ups with Old Parchment. Highlight here and there with Light Ivory.

HAIR: Using the #2 liner, basecoat with Old Parchment. To achieve a variety of hair shades, you can apply a thin wash of Rouge to change the colour slightly for a couple of angels. Shade with strokes of Palomino Tan, adding a touch of Rouge to the Palomino Tan where desired. Highlight with strokes of Light Ivory.

HATS: Basecoat each hat with a different shade of red: paint a couple of them Barn Red + Rouge, then for others mix in some Palomino Tan, Old Parchment or Light Ivory to change the colour slightly. Float shading on darker hats with Barn Red + a touch of Blue Velvet and shade lighter ones with Barn Red. Float highlights on each one with a lighter tone of your choice. Add

(Continued on Page 38)

Celebration!

Match and attach with the pattern section on page 38

Celebration!

Match and attach with the pattern
section on pages 36-37

Celebration!
(Continued from Page 36)

decorations of your choice. Ribbons are painted with thinned Rouge.

INSTRUMENTS

Basecoat the horns and front of the guitar with Palomino Tan.

HORNS: The shadows and highlights should have sharp edges, not floated. Use a liner or a small round brush for the smaller instruments and a #4 round brush for the large horn. Apply shading in layers with Walnut. Start with thinned paint for the first layer, then darken gradually.

Highlight first with strokes of Old Parchment. Apply a thin wash of Walnut on some of the highlights to soften. Add smaller, sharp highlights with Light Ivory. The flute has little "holes" of Blue Velvet.

GUITAR: Basecoat arm and side with a mix of Barn Red + Walnut (1:1). Float around the front with Rouge; repeat until satisfactory. Transfer the detail. The hole, stripes around the hole and hand rest are Blue Velvet. The bar for the strings is Walnut. Strings, keys and fasteners are painted with thinned Old Parchment.

To highlight, drybrush some Old Parchment on the centre of the wider part of the front. Outline the front with Blue Velvet.

FIREWORKS

It would be a good idea to practice this on some other surface first. Use the 3/4" wash brush for larger "bursts" and the #12 flat brush for the others. Sideload the brush with Palomino Tan. Use the chisel edge of the brush to create little lines radiating from the middle (with colour side of the brush toward the centre). Add a touch of Barn Red to the corner of the brush for some of the "bursts." Sideload the brush with Light Ivory for the last layer.

Trail lines for fireworks, some dots and all notes are Palomino Tan. Add more dots, and dot the centres of "bursts" with Light Ivory.

FINISHING TOUCHES

Add the line border with 14K Gold (refer to carpenter's trick in the "General Instructions").

Ornaments

Measure approximately 5/8" (1 1/2 cm) from the edge of the ornaments and mark a line, following the shape of the edge. Stipple this border in the same manner as for the rim of the plate. Trim with 14K Gold, using your choice of strokes. If more opaque strokes and lines are desired, paint them first with Palomino Tan, then over-stroke with the gold.

Reduce pattern to 80% of original and then follow instructions for figures, notes and dots, using the same colours as for the plate.

FINISH AND ENJOY!